ISIS: HARD QUESTIONS WE MUST ASK OURSELVES AND OUR SOCIETY

A MONOLOGUE

BY
VICTOR INGRID

TABLE OF CONTENTS

Acknowledgement 3

Introduction 4

Chapter 1: Questions we must ask ourselves 13

Chapter 2: Questions we must ask ourselves as a society 21

Chapter 3: Eliminating ISIS – The Strategy 30

About the Author 42

ACKNOWLEDGEMENT

A special thanks to the men and women, who defend the world against the evil-doers (ISISs) of the world.

INTRODUCTION

The American people first came to know about the Islamist State when an innocent American Citizen was murdered on camera, just because the perpetrators of the heinous act wanted to send a message to the US Government.

It's not like the world did not know about the ISIS menace. Even some Americans knew, but as is the case, for months the ISIS Terror brigade received no attention from the media. Some leaked videos did make their way out of Syria, when ISIS was still in its infancy, and not even one media person raised a finger at the barbarism that was taking place in Syria.

This text is not going to point any fingers at the government, for there are more serious questions that we must first ask ourselves. I was among

THOSE PEOPLE WHO ACCIDENTLY STUMBLED UPON SOME BEHEADING VIDEOS PUT UP BY ISIS WHEN IT WAS STILL NEW.

AND EVEN BACK THEN, I UNDERSTOOD THAT THEY WERE A DIFFERENT KIND OF PROBLEM. AS A NORMAL HUMAN BEING, THE BEST THAT I COULD DO WAS RAISE MY VOICE THROUGH MANY SOURCES. AND THAT IS WHAT I DID. BUT, REALLY WHO WAS LISTENING.

PEOPLE KEPT ON LIVING NORMAL LIVES. EVEN BEFORE THE BEHEADING, PEOPLE WOULD SAY, "THEY ARE NOT OUR PROBLEM. THEY ARE NOT ATTACKING US DIRECTLY." WELL, IF ONE AMERICAN IS ATTACKED, THE WHOLE COUNTRY IS ATTACKED.

IT WASN'T SOME DRUNKEN QUARREL IN DOWNTOWN FALLUJAH, THIS WAS A MAN MURDERED IN COLD BLOOD. AND TODAY, THEY HAVE MURDERED MORE PEOPLE. ARE

WE STILL SAYING, THEY ARE NOT OUR PROBLEM?

I DON'T THINK WE CAN SAY THAT ANYMORE. WE MUST ASK OURSELVES. AND BY WE, I MEAN THE MEDIA SHOULD FIRST ASK ITSELF, WHY IT DID NOT HIGHLIGHT THIS DEMON CALLED ISIS BEFORE? WHY DID WE WAIT FOR A MAN TO DIE, BEFORE WE STARTED TAKING THESE DEVILS SERIOUSLY?

WE MUST ASK OURSELVES. AND BY WE, I MEAN THE AMERICAN PEOPLE, WHO SAW FIRSTHAND THE VIOLENCE AND BRUTALITY METED OUT AT THE HANDS OF THE SYRIAN GOVERNMENT AND THEN BY THE OPPOSING FORCES, ONE OF WHICN WAS ISIS? IF I SAW IT, I AM SURE THE WORLD WAS ALSO SEEING THE BEHEADINGS AND THE BRUTALITIES, ALMOST LIVE, COMMITTED BY THESE PERPETRATORS.

WE MUST ASK OURSELVES. AND BY WE, I MEAN THE REPRESENTATIVES OF THE

PEOPLE, WHY EVEN TODAY, WE ARE RELATIVELY SOFT ON PEOPLE WHO ARE CLEARLY OUR PROBLEM?

WHY HAS A "WAR" BEEN DECLARED ON ISIS SO LATE IN THE GAME, AND WHY DID WE NOT PAY OUR WAY OUT LIKE MANY OTHER COUNTRIES DID, IN ORDER TO GET OUR CITIZENS OUT OF THAT HELL HOLE?

I AM NOT SAYING, THAT IS THE RIGHT WAY, BUT THAT WAS SOMETHING OTHER COUNTRIES HAD DONE, AND IF THAT SAVED LIVES OF THEIR CITIZENS, WHY COULDN'T WE DO THAT FOR OUR OWN?

THERE ARE MORAL ISSUES OF COURSE, WHEN IT COMES TO PAYING A RANSOM. BUT, WE DID NOT EVEN DISCUSS THIS. AND FINALLY.

WE MUST ASK OURSELVES. AND BY WE, I MEAN THE SOCIETY (SOCIETIES ACROSS THE ENGLISH SPEAKING WORLD), WHY ARE OUR

YOUTH, SO EASILY MISGUIDED BY THESE
DEVILS TO JOIN THEIR "CAUSE".

HOW DO THESE PEOPLE BRAINWASH YOUNG
MEN AND WOMEN, TO THE EXTENT THAT
THEY ARE READY TO LEAVE THEIR OWN
HOMES, AND THEIR OWN SOCIETY, TO GO
JOIN A WAR, WHICH WILL MOST LIKELY LEAD
TO THEIR END?

AND WE MUST ASK OURSELVES, HOW WE
CAN OUR OWN PEOPLE FROM PASSING ON
TO THE DARK SIDE? AND HOW TO BRING
THE PEOPLE WHO HAVE ALREADY CROSSED,
BACK INTO OUR SOCIETY?

OF COURSE, IT IS NOW QUESTIONABLE THAT
ANYONE WHO HAS SEEN SO MUCH VIOLENCE
WOULD EVER BE ABLE TO RETURN TO CIVIL
SOCIETY, STILL IT IS OUR DUTY TO TRY.

MY QUESTIONS MAY SEEM SHARP. TO
SOME, MY QUESTIONS MAY SEEM

CONTROVERSIAL. BUT, MY INTENTION IS NOT TO CREATE CONTROVERSY.

MY INTENTION IS TO ENSURE THAT WE ACCEPT THE FACT THAT THERE ARE SOME FAULTS WITHIN OUR OWN SYSTEM AND SOCIETY, WHICH HAVE ALLOWED DEVILISH ARMIES SUCH AS ISIS TO GROW.

I MEAN THE QUESTIONS ABOVE ARE INTERNATIONAL IN NATURE. IT'S NOT JUST AMERICAN MEDIA, THE BRITISH MEDIA WASN'T SO KEEN ON PUSHING NEWS ABOUT ISIS AT FIRST EITHER.

IN FACT, NONE OF THE GREAT NAMES IN MEDIA, IN THE WESTERN WORLD OR IN THE EASTERN WORLD PAID ANY HEED TO THIS MENACE CALLED ISIS.

AND YET, RECENTLY WE HAVE SEEN THE BRITISH PREMIER HAVING TO TACKLE THE POTENTIAL PROBLEM IN HIS COUNTRY RELATED TO ISIS.

We have also seen the Chinese government basically disown its citizens who have joined IS. We have heard the US government finally declare a war on the Islamic State.

We must accept, IS is a global menace, and it has successfully attracted youth from across the world. We have to face the reality today, that something must be driving young minds into battle. And we must find a solution, which would eradicate this problem once and for all.

This text provides some solutions, based on past instances where terrorism or terrorist ideology was successfully eliminated from a part of society.

All in all, we will hold ourselves accountable, identify problems, lay out solutions, and then hope that we

ACT TOWARDS ELIMINATING THE MENACE CALLED ISIS.

CHAPTER 1: QUESTIONS WE MUST ASK OURSELVES AS INDIVIDUALS AND THINK TANKS

ALTHOUGH, I HAVE ALREADY LAID OUT SOME OF THE QUESTIONS. SOME DEEPER AND MORE DISTURBING QUESTIONS STILL PERVADE MY MIND.

THE FIRST QUESTION THAT COMES TO MIND IS: KNOWING FULL WELL THAT PEOPLE WERE BEING MASSACRED IN SYRIA, BOTH BY THE GOVERNMENT AS WELL AS BY THE REBELS, WHY DID WE NOT ACT?

WE, WHO REFUSE TO LET ANY COUNTRY OR LEADER MASSACRE ITS OWN PEOPLE, WHY DID WE NOT ACT IN SYRIA, WHEN CLEARLY, FOR MONTHS, ABHORRENT VIDEOS KEPT SURFACING ON SOCIAL MEDIA, SHOWING THE BRUTALITY AND SUFFERING INFLICTED BY THE GOVERNMENT THERE?

THE INHUMAN NATURE OF ISIS, HAS NOT BEEN CONCEIVED OUT OF FUN OR SADISTIC NATURE. A SYSTEMATIC MASSACRE OF THE SYRIAN PEOPLE TOOK PLACE, IN FRONT OF THE WORLD, FOR MONTHS.

THAT INHUMAN VIOLENCE, HAD TO RESULT IN SOME SORT OF A REACTION FROM THE PEOPLE. FACED WITH INHUMAN TORTURE, SOME PEOPLE RAISED THEIR VOICES AND WERE QUICKLY SILENCED.

THIS OPPRESSION RESULTED IN AN EVEN MORE VIOLENT, MORE SATANIC REBELLION. BORN OUT OF THIS REBELLION WERE MANY FACTIONS, THE MOST BARBARIC AMONG THEM WAS ISIS.

OF COURSE, PEOPLE MAY ARGUE ABOUT MY STORY ABOUT THE BIRTH OF ISIS. BUT, WHAT WE CANNOT IGNORE IS THE SIMPLE FACT THAT INHUMANITY CREATED INHUMANITY. HAD WE ACTED IN ANY WAY, SHAPE OR FORM, PERHAPS THERE WOULD BE NO ISIS.

BUT WAIT!

HERE COMES MY SECOND QUESTION.

WE DID ACT. WE DECIDED TO SUPPLY ARMS AND AMMUNITIONS TO THE REBELS, INCLUDING ISIS. AND AS HAD BEEN DONE IN IRAQ AND AFGHANISTAN IN THE 80S AND 90S, WE OVER SUPPLIED WEAPONRY.

SO MUCH SO THAT, INSTEAD OF CREATING A DETERRING FORCE, WE COMPLETELY TIPPED THE SCALE IN FAVOR OF ONE SIDE, AT THE HELM OF THIS RISING SIDE? WAS ISIS.

OF COURSE, IT MUST HAVE BEEN WITH GREAT DEAL OF INTELLIGENCE, INFORMATION AND DEBATE, THAT SUCH AN ACTION WAS TAKEN.

BUT THAT JUST LEADS TO MY SECOND QUESTION:

WHY DID WE NOT ACT ONCE WE REALIZED THAT THE SITUATION HAD GOTTEN OUT OF CONTROL?

WERE THERE NO SIGNS BEFORE THE AMERICAN CITIZEN WAS BEHEADED? DID WE NOT SEE THAT ISIS DECIDED TO SPREAD ITS INFLUENCE INTO IRAQ? AND BY INFLUENCE I MEAN TERROR.

AND NOW ON TO MY THIRD AND FINAL QUESTION.

BACK WHEN 9/11 HAPPENED, I WAS IN INDIA. I REMEMBER THAT DAY VIVIDLY. IT WAS EVENING THERE AND I HAD JUST SWITCHED ON THE TV BECAUSE IT WAS TIME FOR F.R.I.E.N.D.S.

BUT, WHEN I SWITCHED IT ON, "SKY NEWS" WAS FLASHING A VIDEO OF THE FIRST TRADE TOWER HIT.

NORMAL TELECAST HAD BEEN DISRUPTED TO SHOW THIS HORRIFIC INCIDENT. BEFORE I COULD EVEN GET UP TO CALL ANYBODY, TO MY HORROR, ANOTHER PLANE CAME IN AND JUST HIT THE SECOND TOWER.

AND THE CAMERA WAS IN SUCH A PERFECT ANGLE THAT I SAW IT AS IF I WAS THERE. WITHIN SECONDS, THE JOURNALIST CHANGED HIS NEWS PITCH — "THIS IS A TERROR ATTACK. I REPEAT, THIS IS A TERROR ATTACK."

OF COURSE, THE REST AS THEY SAY IS TRAGIC HISTORY.

FOR A MOMENT, LET US FORGET ABOUT THE WARS THAT FOLLOWED THIS HORRIFIC ACT. LET US FOCUS ON US SOIL.

THOUSANDS WERE DETAINED, QUESTIONED, OR HARASSED, JUST BECAUSE THEY WERE OF A CERTAIN COLOR AND RACE (NOT EVEN RELIGION).

THOSE ASSOCIATED WITH THAT PARTICULAR RELIGION, WERE SUBJECTED TO OTHER KIND OF TREATMENTS AS WELL. BUT, THE FACT IS, A VISIBLE RACIAL PROFILING WAS DONE.

AND WHAT WAS THE RESULT? WERE WE ABLE TO PREVENT ATTACKS?

THE UNFORTUNATE BOSTON MARATHON BOMBING WAS CARRIED OUT BY CAUCASIAN MEN. NO DOUBT THERE RELIGION WAS ISLAM, BUT THEY WERE WHITE AND HENCE WERE ABLE TO ESCAPE UNDER THE RADAR, WHICH WAS BUSY SCANNING PEOPLE FROM A CERTAIN RACE.

DAVID HEADLEY WAS ARRESTED BY THE FBI, HE APPEARED CAUCASIAN AND WAS AT ONE TIME EVEN AN INFORMANT FOR THE DEA!

WHEN HE WAS ARRESTED, HE IMMEDIATELY STARTED CO-OPERATING, BUT THE JUDGE STILL SENTENCED HIM TO 35 YEARS IN PRISON.

THERE ARE NUMEROUS OTHER SUCH CASES. AND SO MUST AGAIN ASK OURSELVES, WAS RACIAL PROFILING THE REAL SOLUTION?

What did we actually achieve on the ground? What answer should we give to the families of those who were killed in Mumbai Attacks caused by Headley, including the Americans in the Taj hotel?

What answer should we give to the families of the men who were beheaded by a visibly British citizen (acting for ISIS)? Clearly, the problem runs deeper that skin color in the world. And we must look for other solutions.

So, my final question is, was it Racial Arrogance, that made us look the other way when people who were Caucasians or African-Americans, were visibly propagating or aiding or causing terrorism?

And what is the solution?

CHAPTER 2: QUESTIONS WE MUST ASK OURSELVES AS A SOCIETY

A FEW YEARS AGO, RIOTS BROKE OUT IN THE UK. YOUNG PEOPLE IN THEIR TEENS AND 20S, LOOTED, VANDALIZED AND IN A FEW CASES KILLED PEOPLE, FOR NO REASON.

THE THEN PM, DAVID CAMERON, WHO BY THE WAY IS AN IMPRESSIVE LEADER, SAID:

"BUT CRIME HAS A CONTEXT. AND WE MUST NOT SHY AWAY FROM IT...

HERE IS A MAJOR PROBLEM IN OUR SOCIETY WITH CHILDREN GROWING UP NOT KNOWING THE DIFFERENCE BETWEEN RIGHT AND WRONG...

A CULTURE THAT GLORIFIES VIOLENCE, SHOWS DISRESPECT TO AUTHORITY, AND SAYS EVERYTHING ABOUT RIGHTS BUT NOTHING ABOUT RESPONSIBILITIES...

CONSEQUENCES OF NEGLECT AND IMMORALITY ON THIS SCALE HAVE BEEN

CLEAR FOR TOO LONG, WITHOUT ENOUGH ACTION BEING TAKEN…"

THERE IS VERY SPECIFIC REASON WHY I HAVE PLACED THIS EXCERPT HERE. A LEADER OF A NATION, OPENLY ADMITTING THE PROBLEM IN SOCIETY! HERE IS THE OFFICIAL LINK TO THE COMPLETE STATEMENT BY MR. CAMERON: LINK.

THE PROBLEMS FACED BY THE UK BACK THEN, AND EVEN TODAY, ARE IN NO WAY DIFFERENT THAT THE PROBLEMS SOCIETY AND HUMANITY ACROSS THE WORLD FACES.

TIME AND AGAIN, EACH COUNTRY HAS HAD ITS SHARES OF RIOTS AND VIOLENCE, WHICH HAD NOTHING TO DO WITH ANY CAUSE. PEOPLE RIOT, LOOT, KILL, INJURE- JUST FOR FUN. KIDS SHOOT OTHER KIDS IN SCHOOL, BECAUSE THEY HAVE ACCESS TO HIGH POWERED WEAPONS.

YOUNG PEOPLE NOT FULLY UNDERSTANDING THE CONSEQUENCES OF THEIR ACTIONS, RUNNING OF AND JOINING TERRORIST ORGANIZATIONS.

THERE IS SOMETHING SERIOUSLY WRONG WITH SOCIETY, AND CAMERON'S SPEECH CAPTURES THE REASONS QUITE EFFECTIVELY.

SO HERE IS MY FIRST QUESTION: WHAT COULD CAUSE A YOUNG, LITERATE, TECH SAVVY, INTELLIGENT, WELL-BRED, INDIVIDUAL TO JOIN A FANATIC ORGANIZATION SUCH AS ISIS?

WHY DOES IT COME AS A SURPRISE TO PARENTS WHEN THEIR KIDS ARE FOUND GUILTY OF WRONG DOING? (AS WAS THE CASE WITH THE TWO MEN INVOLVED IN THE BOSTON MARATHON BOMBINGS)

THE CAUSE? AS ANY PSYCHOLOGIST WORTH HIS SALT WOULD TELL YOU- THE YOUNG

MIND IS IMPRESSIONABLE. IT'S EASIER TO MOLD YOUNG PEOPLE, WHICH IS WHY BOKO HARAM (THE OTHER ISIS IN THE WORLD) RECRUITS KIDS AS YOUNG AS 9!

BUT, THE DIFFERENCE BETWEEN THE YOUTH WHO ARE RECRUITED BY BOKO HARAM AND THE YOUTH RECRUITED BY ISIS, IS THAT THE FORMER HAVE NO CHOICE IN THE MATTER, WHEREAS THE LATTER DO!

SO, WHAT THEN PULLS THESE INTELLIGENT YOUNG MEN INTO JOINING TERRORISTS? IT IS THE SIMPLE BUT EFFECTIVE STRATEGY USED BY EVERY POWERFUL COUNTRY IN THE WORLD, PROPAGANDA!

NOT ONLY IS FALSE AND INFLAMMATORY CONTENT AVAILABLE ON THE WEB, IT IS READILY AVAILABLE TO THE IMPRESSIONABLE YOUTH.

AND YES, THERE ARE CERTAINLY SOME CHECKS PUT IN PLACE TO STOP THIS KIND OF ACTIVITY, BUT THIS IS NOT ENOUGH.

HATE-MONGERING BOOKLETS, PRINTOUTS, AND AUDIOS MAKE THEIR WAY INTO THE HANDS OF TEENAGERS. AND, SUCH CONTENT INCITES THESE YOUNGSTERS TO TAKE UP ARMS IN THE NAME OF RELIGION OR IN THIS CASE A RELIGION-BASED CALIPHATE.

SO HERE IS MY SECOND QUESTION:

WHAT IS THE WAY TO STOP SUCH CONTENT FROM INFECTING YOUNG MINDS?

WE MUST ALL SEEK A SOLUTION TO THIS MAMMOTH PROBLEM.

WE MUST ASK OURSELVES, SHOULD WE PUT MORE CHECKS ON THE CONTENT THAT REACHES YOUNG MINDS?

I MEAN, WHEN SOME SEXUAL-PREDATOR CAN BE TRACKED WHEN HE STARTS LOOKING FOR HIS NEXT TEN YEAR OLD VICTIM, CAN WE NOT DO THE SAME THING FOR TRACKING AND STOPPING INFLAMMATORY RELIGIOUS CONTENT?

WE MUST ALSO ASK OURSELVES WHERE TO STOP WITH SUCH AN INFORMATION BLOCKADE?

BECAUSE WE CERTAINLY DON'T WANT TO STOP RELIGIONS FROM FLOURISHING FREELY, BUT WE DO WANT TO ENSURE THAT EVEN WRONG SUBTLE MESSAGES DON'T REACH IMPRESSIONABLE MINDS.

THEN, THERE IS ALSO THE QUESTION OF HOW TO STOP SOMEONE FROM CREATING TEXT AND PRINTING IT OUT? IS THERE A WAY TO STOP?

CAN WE HAVE EYES AND EARS ON THE GROUND? SHOULD WE TRY TO INVOLVE

PEOPLE BELOW 30, TO ACT AS INFORMANTS, ACROSS SCHOOLS AND COLLEGES? I DON'T THINK SO. THIS WOULD BE A BAD IDEA.

BUT THEN, WHAT IS A WAY TO STOP PEOPLE FROM CROSSING OVER TO THE DARK SIDE? PERHAPS A BETTER OPTION LIES IN OUR SOURCES OF ENTERTAINMENT.

TV SHOWS, MOVIES AND BOOKS, MAY BE USED, AS THEY HAVE IN THE PAST TO CREATE A MORALLY BETTER SOCIETY.

TOO MUCH OF "THE PRINCE" VALUE SYSTEM HAS PERVADED INTO OUR SOCIAL PSYCHE DUE TO ENTERTAINMENT CONTENT OFFERING MACHIAVELLIAN SOLUTIONS TO LIFE'S PROBLEMS.

PERHAPS IT IS TIME AGAIN TO LOOK AT THIS SOLUTION, FOR IT IS CERTAINLY BETTER THAN STOPPING THE FLOW OF

INFORMATION OR SPYING ON OUR OWN PEOPLE.

ULTIMATELY, MOVIES REFLECT REALITY. BUT, IT ALSO TRUE THE OTHER WAY ROUND. PERHAPS, IF WE TUNED DOWN THE "BEG, BORROW, STEAL, LIE, CHEAT" MODEL AND REVVED UP THE "FIGHT JUSTLY AND WIN" MODEL ON OUR TELEVISION SHOWS, THINGS WOULD IMPROVE. AGAIN THIS IS ONLY CONJECTURE.

SO, MY QUESTIONS ABOVE STILL STAND UNANSWERED. IF I REALLY HAD THE ANSWERS, I WOULDN'T BE ASKING THE QUESTIONS, WOULD I?

CHAPTER 3: ELIMINATING ISIS – THE STRATEGY

And, so. Finally, we have reached the point in this text where we look at eliminating the elephant in the room.

We can talk about changing our society long after ISIS is gone from this world.

But, today, facing us is this demon, which has its roots in a world which encourages violence and a world where being a person of another faith could get you beheaded!

So, how can we eliminate ISIS and other such organizations? You see, today when impressionable youngsters are joining the devilish organizations, merely killing the leaders and conducting air strikes would just not do. The war has come to us.

THIS IS NOT A WAR OF WEAPONS. THIS IS NOT A WAR OF WORDS. THIS IS NOT A WAR OF FAITHS. THIS IS A WAR OF IDEOLOGIES!

AND THAT IS WHERE WE ARE NOT EVEN PUTTING UP A FIGHT. EVERY DAY, THAT ISIS SURVIVES WE LOSE THIS WAR OF THE IDEOLOGIES.

OUR IDEOLOGY PERMITS FREEDOM OF SPEECH AND OF ACTION. IT ALLOWS FOR RELIGIOUS TOLERANCE. WE ARE FREE TO DEBATE EVEN THE MOST DIFFICULT OF ISSUES, AND FIND SOLUTIONS BY WAY OF WORDS AND NOT WEAPONS.

THEIR IDEOLOGY DOES NOT ALLOW FOR FREE SPEECH. IT DOES NOT ALLOW RELIGIOUS TOLERANCE. THERE ARE NO DEBATES. EITHER YOU JOIN THEM OR YOU DIE. SOLUTIONS ARE FOUND THERE, BY WAY OF WEAPONS AND NOT BY WORDS.

OUR IDEOLOGY ALLOWS FOR CIVILITY. EVEN OUR ARMIES, DON'T LOOT, PLUNDER AND RAPE. THEY ARE PROFESSIONAL ARMIES, WHICH DEFEND SOVEREIGN NATIONS AGAINST OPPOSING FORCES. PEOPLE IN OUR PRISONS STILL GET TREATED LIKE HUMANS (ALBEIT BAD ONES). LET US PUT ASIDE GUANTANAMO BAY. AND, TILL THE VERY LAST MOMENT, WE TRY TO TALK IT OUT WITH THE ENEMY BEFORE EVEN FIRING A SINGLE BULLET.

THEIR IDEOLOGY DOES NOT CONTAIN EVEN A FRACTION OF CIVILITY. THE UNPROFESSIONAL BARBARIC DEVILS KILL CHILDREN AND RAPE WOMEN. THEY FORCE FAMILIES TO SUBMIT YOUNG PEOPLE INTO THEIR SERVICE, AND FORCE WOMEN TO MARRY AGAINST WILL. THEY TAKE NO PRISONERS, AS IS EVIDENT FROM THE INNUMERABLE VIDEOS AVAILABLE. THEY ONLY TAKE PRISONERS, IF THEY SEE SOME BENEFIT — PERHAPS A HOPE OF RANSOM, OR

A WAY TO DETER WORLD POWERS OF
TAKING ACTION.

OUR IDEOLOGY, ALLOWS FOR FREEDOM OF
CHOOSING A LIFE WE WANT. WHETHER YOU
WANT TO BE A HIPPY OR A SCIENTIST,
WHETHER YOU BELIEVE IN MERMAIDS OR
CHOOSE TO HUNT ALIENS, WHETHER YOU
CHOOSE TO DRESS UP OR DRESS DOWN. THE
LAWS YOU FOLLOW ARE THE SAME FOR ALL,
BECAUSE WE BELIEVE IN EQUALITY.

THEIR IDEOLOGY ASKS THAT YOU CHOOSE A
LIFE THEY WANT. FALL IN LINE, OR FALL
INTO THE ABYSS. YOUR ATTIRE MUST BE AS
DEFINED BY THEM. AND THE LAWS ARE NOT
THE SAME FOR ALL. "NON-BELIEVERS"
DON'T SEE THE LIGHT OF DAY. THERE IS NO
CONCEPT OF EQUALITY. I DON'T EVEN THINK
HALF THE PEOPLE FIGHTING FOR ISIS
KNOW, WHAT THE END GOAL REALLY IS FOR
THEM.

FINALLY, OUR IDEOLOGY ALLOWS US TO ASK QUESTIONS. WE CAN QUESTION OUR LEADERS ABOUT THEIR DECISIONS. WE CAN HOLD THEM ACCOUNTABLE. WE CAN WRITE A TEXT AS THE ONE I AM WRITING RIGHT NOW, AND LET PEOPLE READ IT. WE CAN RAISE OUR VOICES IN A MILLION DIFFERENT WAYS.

THEIR IDEOLOGY DOES NOT ALLOW QUESTIONING OF LEADERS. NO ONE CAN HOLD ANYONE ACCOUNTABLE. IF I WAS WRITING THIS TEXT UNDER THEIR REGIME, IT WOULD NEVER BE ABLE TO REACH YOUR HANDS. PEOPLE CANNOT RAISE THEIR VOICES, AND THOSE WHO TRY, LOSE THEIR NECKS AND THEIR VOICES.

NOW THAT I HAVE GENTLY PLACED THE DIFFERENCES IN THE IDEOLOGIES. LET ME MOVE FORWARD AND SAY, THAT SINCE THIS IS A WAR OF IDEOLOGIES, WE MUST WIN IT BY SPREADING OUR MESSAGE CLEARLY AS WELL.

WE MUST ELIMINATE THE CONCEPT OF SOME CALIPHATE, BEFORE WE EVEN BEGIN TO ELIMINATE THE PEOPLE BEHIND THE CONCEPT.

HOW DO WE REMOVE THE CONCEPT? HOW DO WE KILL THE IDEOLOGY?

POSITIVE REALITY FOR ONE. PROPAGANDA FOR ANOTHER. WE CAN CAPTURE AIR WAVES AND HIJACK SIGNALS, TO ENSURE THAT THE SAME WAY WE WERE ABLE TO GET THE MESSAGES OUT OF SYRIA, WE ARE ABLE TO GET MESSAGES INTO THE ISIS STRONGHOLD.

WE MUST ALSO BREAK THE BACK OF THEIR IDEOLOGY ON OUR OWN LANDS AS WELL. TOO LONG HAVE WE IGNORED THE RELIGION AND RELIGIOUS LEADERS.

TOO LONG HAVE WE SIDELINED MEN OF GOD AND THEIR SERMONS. IF A CHRISTIAN

WERE TO LECTURE JEWS OR MUSLIMS ON THEIR RELIGIONS, OR THEIR DUTIES, DO YOU THINK IT WOULD WORK? IT WOULD NOT.

SO, WE HAVE TO INCLUDE THE LEADERS OF THE RELIGION, UNDER WHOSE GARB, INHUMAN ATROCITIES ARE BEING COMMITTED.

IN THE NAME OF COUNTRY, IN THE NAME OF DUTY, IN THE NAME OF GOD OR BY ANY OTHER MEANS, WE MUST ASK THAT MODERATE RELIGIOUS LEADERS OF VARIOUS FAITHS COME TOGETHER, AND THAT THEY SPREAD THE SAME MESSAGE OF PEACE AMONG THEIR FOLLOWERS.

EXTREMISM HAS A PLACE, AND IT IS ON THE SIDELINES. IMPRESSIONABLE YOUNGSTERS MUST BE MADE TO REALIZE THAT WE LIVE IN THE 21ST CENTURY, WHERE COUNTRIES CANNOT BE CREATED BY MILITARY AGGRESSION.

THE RELIGIOUS LEADERS MUST CITE THEIR OWN HOLY TEXTS, TO CONVEY TO THEIR FOLLOWERS THE TRUE MESSAGE OF GOD.

AS A NON-MUSLIM, I HAVE STILL READ THE QURAN. IN FACT, I HAVE EXPLORED EVERY RELIGION. AND I CAN TELL YOU, NOWHERE IS IT WRITTEN THAT PEOPLE BE MASSACRED.

AND EVEN IF SUCH A THING WERE WRITTEN SOME PLACE, PERHAPS WE SHOULD CHANGE IT OURSELVES. FOR THE MOST MIRACULOUS SITE WAS IT, WHEN THE POPE RECENTLY MARRIED CO-LOCATED MODERN COUPLES. FOR WHEN THE PAPACY CAN CHANGE, SO CAN LEADERS OF OTHER RELIGIONS.

WE LIVE IN A NEW WORLD, AND OUR BATTLES IN THE INFORMATION AGE ARE TO BE FOUGHT AS MUCH IN THE INFORMATION LANDSCAPE, AS THEY ARE TO BE FOUGHT IN THE REAL BATTLEFIELD.

WE MUST ELIMINATE ISIS IDEOLOGY. AND TO DO THAT, WE MUST ENSURE THAT OUR OWN PEOPLE ARE FIRST CONVINCED THAT WHAT WE OFFER IN THE DEMOCRATIC SOVEREIGN NATIONS IS WORTH FIGHTING FOR. BECAUSE IF WE FAIL TODAY, WE WILL REGRET THE CONSEQUENCES FOR MANY GENERATIONS.

ONCE THE IDEOLOGICAL BASE OF THE ISIS IS BROKEN. WE CAN LOOK AT BREAKING THEIR FINANCIAL BACKBONE AS WELL. OF COURSE, THIS IS EASIER THAN ELIMINATING IDEOLOGY AND SINCE WE HAVE MUCH EXPERIENCE IN THIS FIELD, DUE TO OUR PROLONGED YET SUCCESSFUL WAR AGAINST AL-QAEDA, I WILL NOT DELVE DEEPER INTO THIS MATTER.

IT SHALL SUFFICE TO SAY, THAT TODAY, THE FUNDING SOURCES THAT USED TO FUND AL-QAEDA ARE FUNDING ISIS INSTEAD. AND THESE SOURCES MUST BE BLOCKED, FOR NO AMOUNT OF FAITH CAN PUT FOOD IN THE

ISIS ARMY'S STOMACH, NOR PROVIDE BULLETS FOR THE WEAPONS.

FINALLY, ELIMINATING THE ENEMY IS A MILITARY MATTER AND NOT SOMETHING THAT I SHOULD PROVIDE OPINIONS ABOUT. I WOULD ONLY WISH THAT WE CRUSH THE SERPENT'S HEAD SOON.

THE LONGER THEY REMAIN CAPTORS OF GREAT TRACTS OF LAND, THE HARDER IT WOULD BE TO ELIMINATE THE IDEA OF THE CALIPHATE FROM THE MINDS OF THEIR BELIEVERS.

SO THAT IS A THREE-FOLD APPROACH TO ELIMINATING ISIS. AND IT IS THE RESPONSIBILITY OF THE SOVEREIGN NATIONS TO ELIMINATE ISIS AND ITS AFFILIATES IN ITS ENTIRETY.

THE PROBLEM'S SOURCE LAY IN INHUMAN ACTS, AND THE PEOPLE UNDER ISIS RULE ARE LIVING THROUGH HELL. THEY NEED TO

BE LIBERATED. VOTES AND WORDS, NOT WEAPONS, SHOULD DETERMINE THE FATE OF PEOPLE. AND SO WE MUST END THIS MENACE ONCE AND FOR ALL.

BECAUSE, IF WE DON'T, NO ONE ELSE WOULD.

AND WE WILL HAVE AN UNSTABLE MIDDLE EAST, AND THAT CANNOT BE GOOD FOR OUR ECONOMY, OUR PEOPLE AND OUR WORLD. I HOPE WHEN YOU ARE READING THIS BOOK, ISIS IS NO LONGER RELEVANT TO THE WORLD.

GOD BLESS US ALL!

ABOUT THE AUTHOR

The author has spent his life in the pursuit of happiness. His identity remains secret, hence the use of only a first name. It is the author's belief that one should fight against evil in whatever shape or form possible, and so he has written this work with the utmost care to highlight the evil that we face in our world today.